Fill in the dates on the calendar. Mark the holidays and special days. Color the picture.

MARCH

Sunday	Monday	Tuesday	Wednesday	Thursday	Friday	Saturday

Read the finger play poem. Perform the finger movements as you read the poem again. You may wish to complete the finger puppets on the next page to use with the poem. Color the picture.

March
by Gail Aemmer

When March comes in like a lion, a lamb trots out, we hear.
    (Move fingers as if trotting)

But when the lamb comes first, my friend, it's the roar going out that we fear.
    (Move fingers as if running)

So each and every boy and girl should watch as March comes in.
    (Shade eyes with hand as if looking around)

We'll know the way the month might end, if we know the way it begins!

Complete these finger puppets to use with the finger play poem on the preceding page.

1. Color and cut out each finger puppet.
2. Glue or tape the tabs together so that the puppet fits around your finger.

Look-Alike Lions and Lambs

Circle the pictures in each row that look the same. Color the pictures.

Word Search

Use the word list below to locate the hidden words in the word search. The words may appear diagonally, across or down. Color the picture.

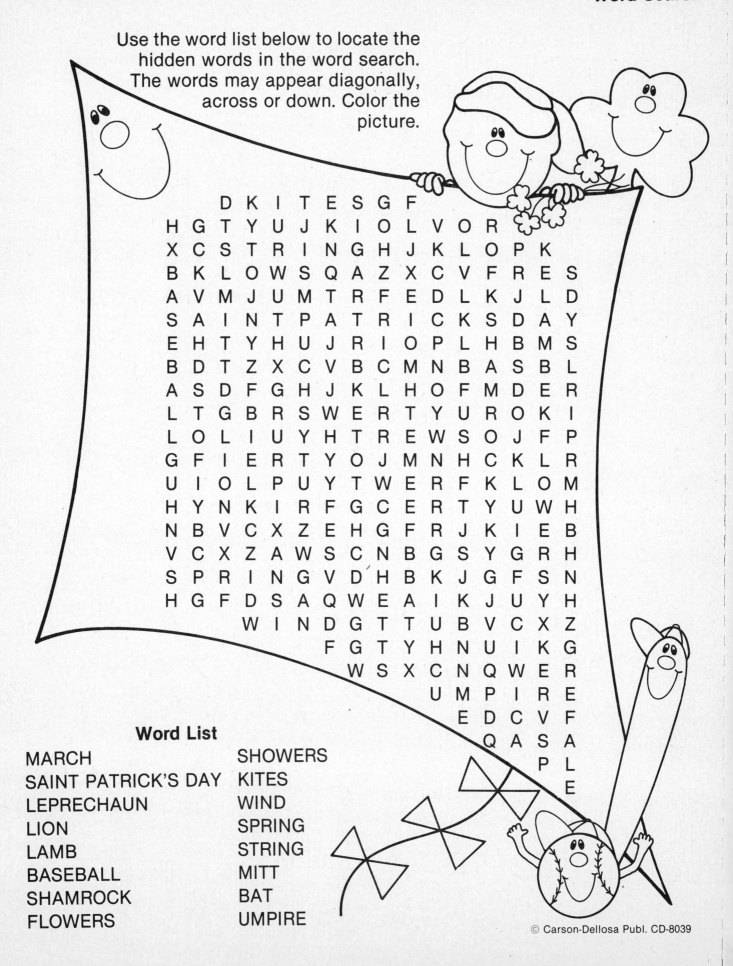

```
          D K I T E S G F
      H G T Y U J K I O L V O R
      X C S T R I N G H J K L O P K
      B K L O W S Q A Z X C V F R E S
      A V M J U M T R F E D L K J L D
      S A I N T P A T R I C K S D A Y
      E H T Y H U J R I O P L H B M S
      B D T Z X C V B C M N B A S B L
      A S D F G H J K L H O F M D E R
      L T G B R S W E R T Y U R O K I
      L O L I U Y H T R E W S O J F P
      G F I E R T Y O J M N H C K L R
      U I O L P U Y T W E R F K L O M
      H Y N K I R F G C E R T Y U W H
      N B V C X Z E H G F R J K I E B
      V C X Z A W S C N B G S Y G R H
      S P R I N G V D H B K J G F S N
      H G F D S A Q W E A I K J U Y H
        W I N D G T T U B V C X Z
        F G T Y H N U I K G
        W S X C N Q W E R E
              U M P I R E F
              E D C V S F A
              Q A S P A L
                    P   E
```

Word List

MARCH
SAINT PATRICK'S DAY
LEPRECHAUN
LION
LAMB
BASEBALL
SHAMROCK
FLOWERS

SHOWERS
KITES
WIND
SPRING
STRING
MITT
BAT
UMPIRE

Materials: paper plate, glue, scissors, crayons

1. Color the rim of the paper plate. This will be the lion's mane.
2. Make cuts around the entire rim of the paper plate. (See example.)
3. Curl the hair forward by rolling each rim section around a pencil.
4. Color and cut out all of the pieces on this page.
5. Glue the ears to the top of the head by placing the ears behind the head. (See example.)
6. Glue the head to the center of the paper plate. (See example.)

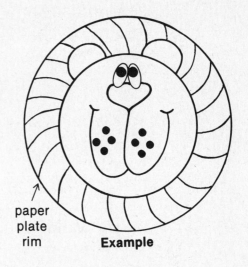

paper plate rim

Example

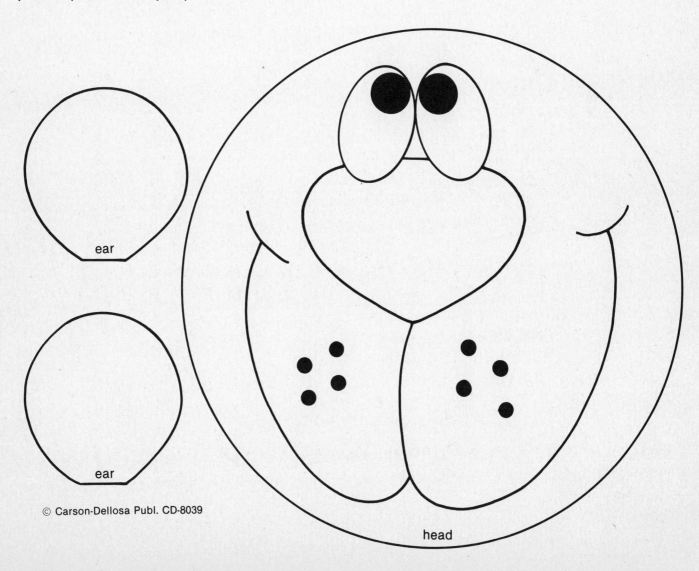

ear

ear

head

Materials: paper plate, glue, scissors, crayons

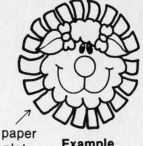

Paper Plate Lamb

1. Make cuts around the entire rim of the paper plate. (See example.) This will be the lamb's wool.
2. Curl the wool forward by rolling each rim section around a pencil.
3. Color and cut out all of the pieces on this page.
4. Glue the ears to the top of the head. (See example.)
5. Glue one bow to each ear. (See example.)
6. Glue the head to the center of the paper plate. (See example.)

paper plate rim

Example

ear

ear

head

St. Patrick's Day Look-Alikes

Circle the pictures in each row that look the same. Color the pictures.

St. Patrick's Day   fortune

leprechaun   shamrock   pot

gold   Irish   lucky

rainbow   emerald

charms

forest   magic

parade

enchanted

clover

hid

green

disappear

holiday

leaf

Use some of the words on the shamrock to write a St. Patrick's Day story on the next page. Color the pictures.

Read the finger play poem. Perform the finger movements as you read the poem again. You may wish to complete the finger puppets on the next page to use with the poem. Color the picture.

Saint Patrick's Day
by Gail Aemmer

Meet Happy John, the leprechaun; he's sort of mad, you'll say.
　　(Hold up one finger, frown)
'Cause he and his brothers can't agree about Saint Patrick's Day.

Now Mack, it's true, is a leprechaun, too; his story must be told.
　　(Hold up 2 fingers)
He says the most important thing is finding the pot o' gold.
　　(Shade eyes with hand, look for gold)

Here's Fred; it's been said he's a leprechaun, that everybody knows.
　　(Hold up three fingers)
Fred says the very best thing is the green on everyone's clothes.
　　(Point to green on clothing or hook thumbs behind imaginary suspenders)

And Cass is last; she says the thing is shamrocks. There's no doubt.
　　(Hold up 4 fingers, bend over to pick shamrock)
'Cause that's the thing Saint Patrick's Day just cannot be without.

You take your pick; we can't decide. They all sound good to us.
　　(Hold up hands, shrug shoulders)
So let's enjoy Saint Patrick's Day and not make such a fuss!
　　(Fold arms; unfold arms, shake index finger)

Complete these finger puppets to use with the finger play poem on the preceding page.

1. Color and cut out each finger puppet.
2. Glue or tape the tabs together so that the puppet fits around your finger.

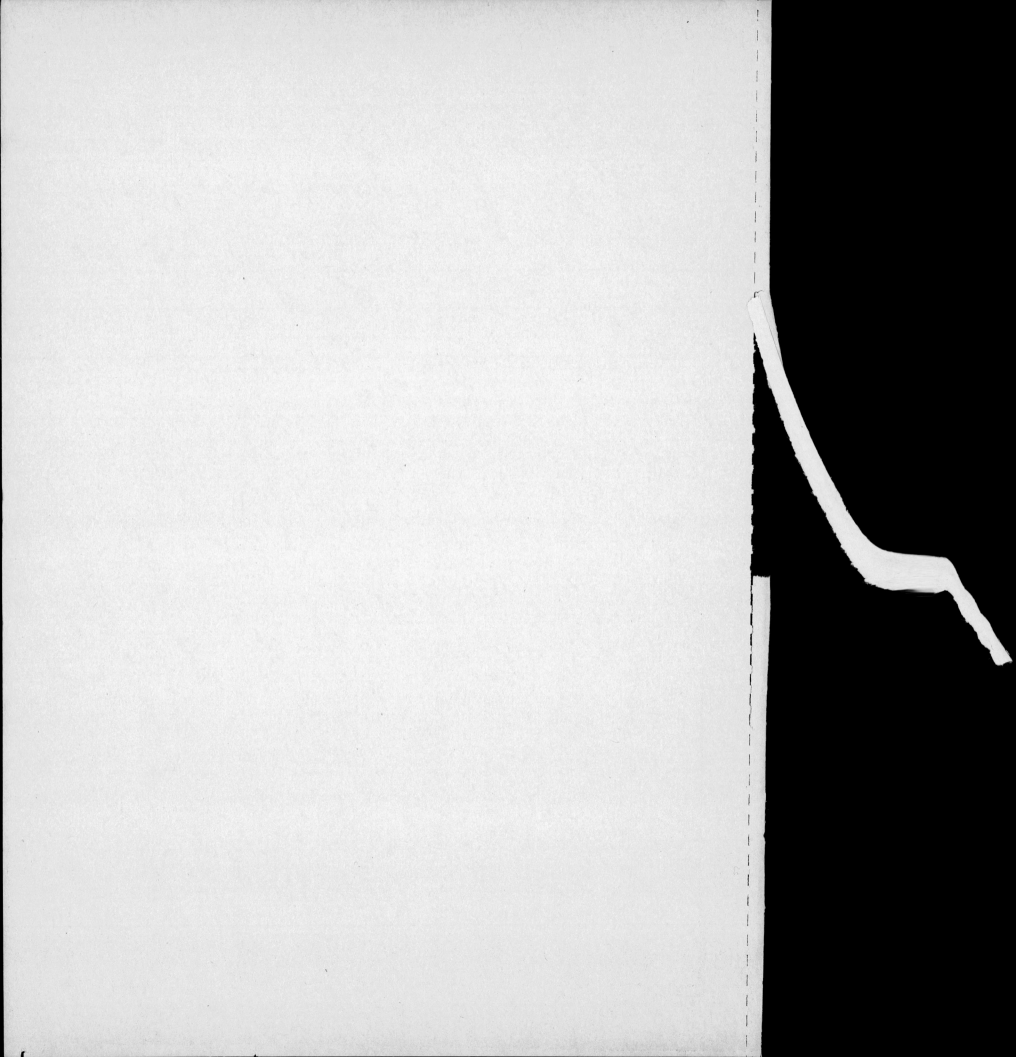

1. Color and cut out all of the pieces.
2. Glue the hat brim to the bottom of the hatband. (See example.)
3. Glue the shamrock to the hatband. (See example.)

Example

shamrock

hat brim

hatband

Circle the pictures in each row that look the same. Color the pictures.

© Carson-Dellosa Publ. CD-8039

Baseball Finger Play Poem

Read the finger play poem. Perform the finger movements as you read the poem again. You may wish to complete the finger puppets on the next page to use with the poem. Color the picture.

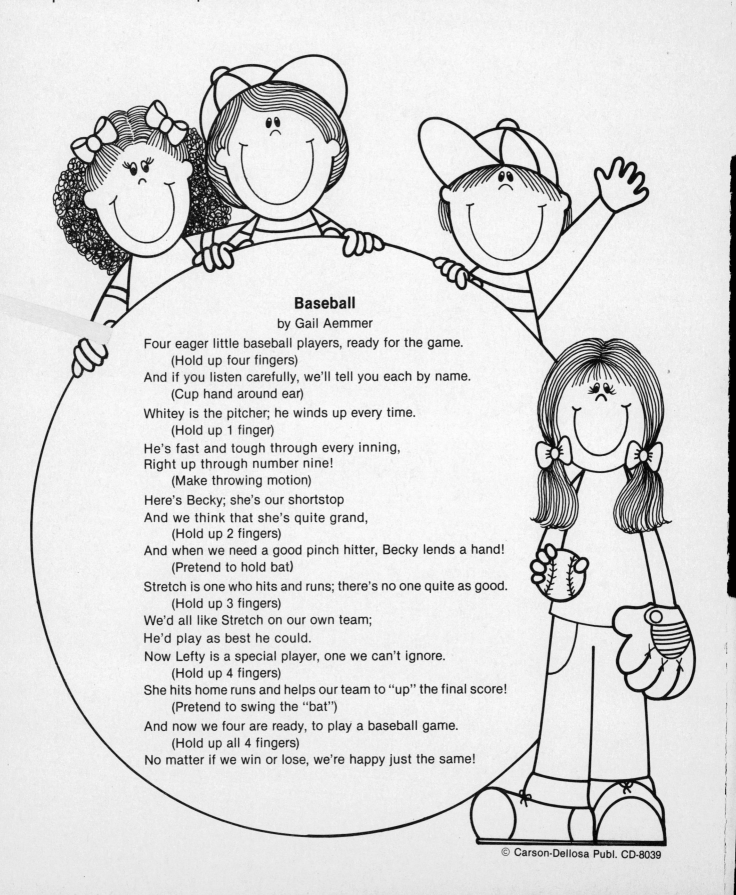

Baseball

by Gail Aemmer

Four eager little baseball players, ready for the game.
  (Hold up four fingers)
And if you listen carefully, we'll tell you each by name.
  (Cup hand around ear)

Whitey is the pitcher; he winds up every time.
  (Hold up 1 finger)
He's fast and tough through every inning,
Right up through number nine!
  (Make throwing motion)

Here's Becky; she's our shortstop
And we think that she's quite grand,
  (Hold up 2 fingers)
And when we need a good pinch hitter, Becky lends a hand!
  (Pretend to hold bat)

Stretch is one who hits and runs; there's no one quite as good.
  (Hold up 3 fingers)
We'd all like Stretch on our own team;
He'd play as best he could.

Now Lefty is a special player, one we can't ignore.
  (Hold up 4 fingers)
She hits home runs and helps our team to "up" the final score!
  (Pretend to swing the "bat")

And now we four are ready, to play a baseball game.
  (Hold up all 4 fingers)
No matter if we win or lose, we're happy just the same!

Complete these finger puppets to use with the finger play poem on the preceding page.

1. Color and cut out each finger puppet.
2. Glue or tape the tabs together so that the puppet fits around your finger.

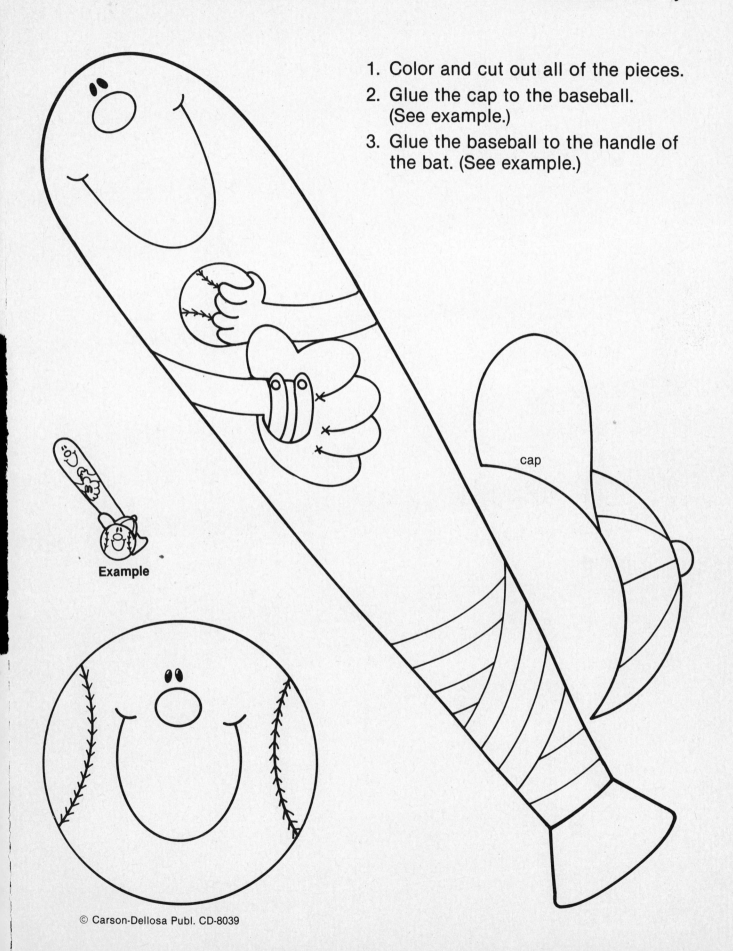

1. Color and cut out all of the pieces.
2. Glue the cap to the baseball. (See example.)
3. Glue the baseball to the handle of the bat. (See example.)

cap

Example

Kite Look-Alikes

Circle the pictures in each row that look the same. Color the pictures.

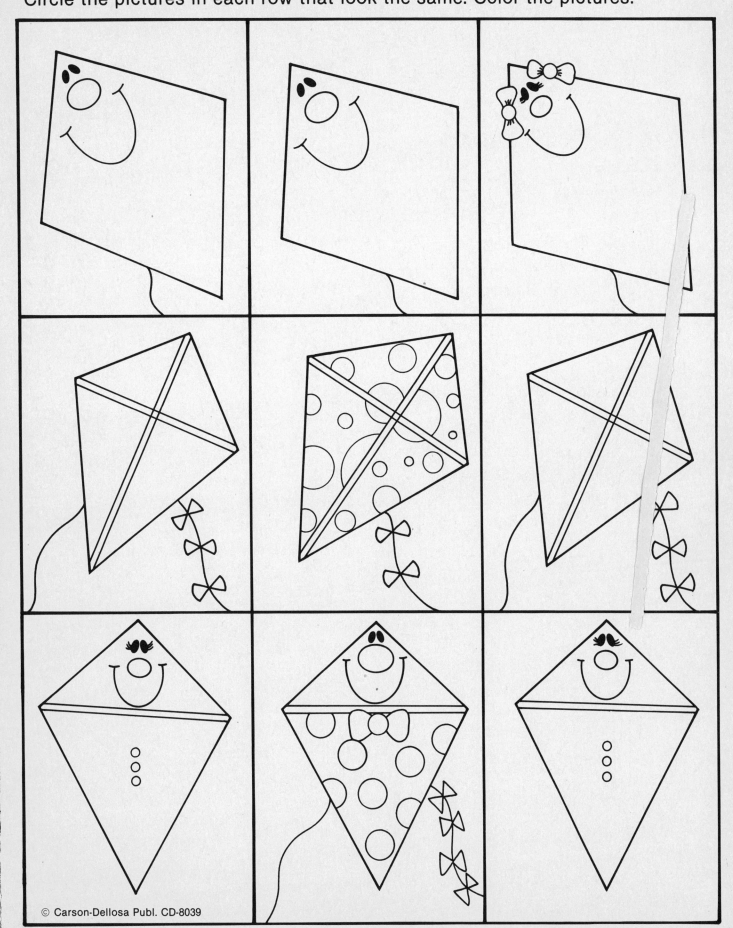

Kites Finger Play Poem

Read the finger play poem. Perform the finger movements as you read the poem again. You may wish to complete the finger puppets on the next page to use with the poem. Color the picture.

Kites

by Gail Aemmer

Kites, kites, so many kites, to sail and glide and soar.
   (Glide fingers)
Our kites, like birds, they float and fly;
We must do this some more!
Our dragon kite is quite a sight.
It's green and has two eyes.
   (Hold up 1 finger)
This butterfly has reached the sky,
Much to our great surprise.
   (Hold up 2 fingers)
This goldfish sort, we must report,
Floats up into the air.
   (Hold up 3 fingers)
Our turkey flier just goes higher;
We take him everywhere!
   (Hold up 4 fingers)
And now our poem about our kites
Is finished and we're done.
We love our kites; our pretty kites,
They're special and they're fun!

Materials: yarn, glue, scissors, crayons

1. Color and cut out all of the pieces.
2. Glue the bow tie to the center line on the kite. (See example.)
3. Glue the nose to the face on the kite. (See example.)
4. Glue a piece of yarn to the bottom of the kite. (See example.)
5. Glue the ties to the yarn. (See example.)

Example

tie

tie

tie

tie

kite

nose

bow tie

Bookmarks

1. Color and cut out all of the bookmarks.
2. Use the bookmarks to mark your place in a book wherever you stop reading.

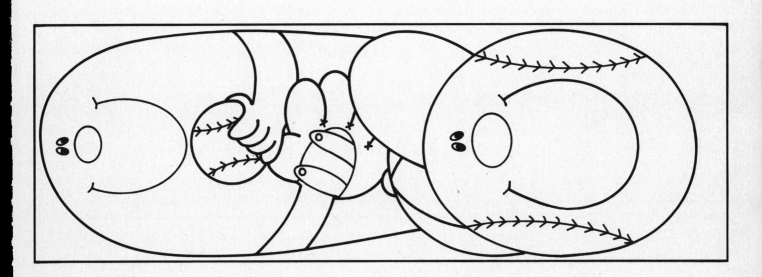